Gone through the

Fire,

Came Out Unsinged

Gone through the

Fire,

Came Out Unsinged

Wanda L. Leggett

XULON PRESS

Xulon Press
2301 Lucien Way #415
Maitland, FL 32751
407.339.4217
www.xulonpress.com

Unless otherwise indicated, Scripture quotations taken from the King James Version (KJV) – *public domain.*

Printed in the United States of America

Paperback ISBN-13: 978-1-66283-198-0
Ebook ISBN-13: 978-1-66283-199-7

I would like to dedicate this book to my mom,
Mother Betty R. Cooper.

Table of Contents

Introduction

*T*his is a book of encouragement. I hope it helps someone to have faith, to hold their head up high, and to continue on with life.

My name is Wanda, and I am a Christian woman. In these pages, I am not pushing anything on you, but I am going to tell you that you cannot go through life without knowing and believing in the one who loves us all. I am writing this book because the almighty Father instructed me to share these words with you. It is my desire to be an encourager, to let people know that life can be great even if you have some setbacks. We know setbacks do happen, but as you read through this book, my hope and prayer is that you will see how you can believe and be refreshed, knowing that the Lord is with you. There is an old saying that says, "Life is what you make it." You know, the Lord gives us a choice, but He also wants us to live a life so others can see His glory in us. You make the first step; He will make two. Praying for your encouragement.

Chapter 1

When God Chooses You

*Y*ou know, it is a wonderful feeling to have the Great I Am choose you to show Himself to others. He has blessed you and wants you to share Him with the world. God knew every one of us by our names way before He even formed us in the womb. He also knew the godly gifts He would give each of us. My gifts are to sing and write, although I just found that out several years ago.

God told me to write a book. "Me?" I asked.

"Yes, you," He said, although I did not do it at the time when He wanted. Thankfully, God is so patient. I have always heard it said that if you do not do what the Lord asks of you, He will give it to another. But God can be stubborn too, especially when He wants one of His children to do something. Therefore, He will not leave you alone until you do it. You see, when God has an assignment or mission for you, He will remind you that your assignment or mission is still waiting for you. "Do It" gifts are a blessing, and He will give you the tools to do your mission. God asked me to do this mission thirty years ago, and knowing me, He waited patiently. What a grand God He is to have chosen an assignment for me to complete in His name.

When God gives you a mission, do it. The mission is for you, and if He wants you to do it, He will wait until you do. Do not waste your time or your gifts; we are to show others what we can do through Christ within our lives, and we are to help others see how wonderful life can be in the great family of God. Remember, I said that He knew all of us before we were formed in the womb, so He also knows what mission He has for each of us. The Scripture says, "I can do all things through Christ who strengthens me" (Phil. 4:13).

Chapter 2

Thank God for the Life He Assigned You

*J*esus is the light of the world, and a great light shines brightly all around. I was raised in church, and when I say raised, I mean raised. Growing up in Ohio, my dad was in the military. We had no car, so our mom would make a picnic basket for us to take to church, since we were going to be in church all day and part of the night. She was my birth mom and a great mom—she was a child of God. However, she was strict, and at the time, I did not know her strict raising would help me in life. I went on to sing in the choir, and I also taught Sunday school alongside my mom. All this was in God's plan for my life, although I did not know it. As the saying goes, raise a child up in the Word of God, and he will not depart from it. You know, having Christ in your life and knowing the Word will be a great help in life.

Be mindful of the life He assigned you, not the life of your friend, your son, your mother, or your sister. He assigned this life especially for you. You or I could not possibly handle the life of someone else. Sometimes, we look at others and wonder how our life might be if we were them. Well, we possibly could not handle it. Jesus is the light of the world, enlightening us of what a great life He gave us. The enemy has no power; when we give our lives to Christ and He gives us an assignment, the enemy will try to turn us the other way. However, when you are trusting in the Lord and believing in Him, the life He chose for you will be a blessing for you and others.

The Learning Process

*T*he Lord is so wonderful. He loves all of His children and wants us to try to understand how He desires us to learn about this precious life with which He has blessed us. We are conceived, we are born, and we grow; we are not able to choose our parents, for God chooses them. Love is there. A long time ago, my late pastor, Andrew Crouch, wrote a song titled "There Is No Greater Love than the Lord God Has for You." You see, through all the things that happen in life, and the way our life starts out, how we deal with it is up to us. Life is a learning experience, and having Christ in our life gives us a better way to deal with all that happens.

Let me explain. It took me a long time to see how special I was to the Lord, to realize that I was not an accident; I was meant to be here. Well, my life started out rough. I won't tell you all I went through, but God knew what He was doing. My dad married the wrong woman, and they did not want me. He sent him to a G&C hearing woman, who raised me.

We all go through various things to prepare us for the future, and God is there all the time, guiding us. As I went through a lot in my life, I learned and am still learning how to please God, for this is what we are here for. When I thought I could do without God, my life went south. I had two sons out of wedlock, and I did some things I am not proud of. You know, your head can get so swollen that you forget who you and what the Great I Am can do. My life was a mess, but like I said, I won't share everything. I had to learn to trust Jesus. Years ago, my mom went home to be with Jesus, and I went through some challenges I have never gone through before—a loss of home, a loss of car, and a loss of sense. However, the Lord was with me through it all. I was lost and told Him I was. Yet, Jesus said, "No, you are not. Just trust Me."

God will see you through. My tests have been ongoing, but I know and believe I will be blessed. Trust in the Lord. You will not be disappointed.

Chapter 4

The Creator Is Great

Do you know how great the Master is? We all know He created the universe, as well as our planet especially for us. He made the oceans, the land, and the animals, then He created us. Do you know how wonderful He is? Well, He has done great things for all of those who believe in Him, pray to Him, and trust in Him. He made ways for Moses, Abraham, David, Paul, Job, and many more of His believers and faithful workers. He is very patient and loving. God is all powerful, and He loves us. He has no favorite, although it may seem that way sometimes; His love is so great that He can spread it as wide as the planet upon which we live. Just think of all the things God has done!

I have been on cruises to Alaska, and I was amazed to see whales in person. I've seen them on TV, but it is not the same. It was wonderful to see the ocean, the animals, and the icebergs, all of which our Creator made. Now, He also created us, and even though we may have done crazy things—things that almost destroy what God has created—He loves us and gives us a chance to ask for His forgiveness. He is great just because He is God. We owe Him a debt we cannot pay, yet Jesus did that for us. You know, God is so patient, even when we take the wrong path. Even when things go wrong, He still loves us. Sometimes, we ask, "Where is God in all this mess?" Don't you know He is right there, waiting for your call? When you call on Him in faith, know that you will receive His attention, and He will answer you with what is for you. He is so great that He knows what you need even before you ask Him, and if you do not receive you answer within your desired time, you can be sure that the answer is on the way. .in His time, not yours or mine. In this, He is still great.

Chapter 5

Count Your Blessings

*I*t is so amazing how we get into trouble when we do dumb things. We want this, we want that. .we can't wait upon the Lord to bless us with what we need when we actually need it. What about what we already have, such as the necessities like food, water, and a place to live? Oh yeah, the ability to breathe, to see, to eat, to walk, to even brush our teeth by ourselves. We often forget to call these things blessings. Life itself is a gift and a blessing. Yes, we need certain things to live, but do we appreciate them?

I refer to songs a lot, and I love the song that says, "Count your blessings, name them one by one, count your many blessings, see what God has done." Stop and count your blessings. When you do, I believe you will count so many, not just blessings for the present. Just think about how the Lord has blessed you through the years. .has He stopped? Have you heard the saying, "You cannot see the forest for the trees"? Well, sometimes, I can't see my blessings for the blessings. In other words, God has given us so many blessings that we often can't see them all. .and we will never see them all or be able to count them all. When we are thankful for the blessings we already have, we will be blessed with even more. Isn't that wonderful? I am not bragging. Don't get me wrong, I myself needed to learn how to count my blessings. When I did, God blessed me more. God's blessings are all about being grateful for what we already have. God knows what we need, and He will always bless us accordingly to His riches and glory, how and when we need it. Remember, He knows all.

OK, I am not judging anyone, but I'd like to encourage you to stop and take inventory of what you have. We are reaching for diamonds and gold, while forgetting about the basics of life. I think if we dig into the lives of the super-rich, we would find that they are not happy. Happiness comes from having Christ in your life and being satisfied with what He has given you. Don't get me wrong, I would love for all my bills to be paid, to have a great house and a fancy car, and to have no worries, but even the richest person has worries. So, I am counting my blessings and having faith that God will bless me even more. Besides, my life could be worse, but it is not.

Chapter 6

Trust God, No Matter What

*T*rust in God, no matter what. Trust is putting all of your faith in a person, letting them into all of your inner life. Now, putting your trust in God should be easy because He already knows all about your life. God created you, so you can trust Him. But sometimes, we get so caught up in our lives, especially when things are not going the way we want them to go, and we lose sight of our faith, forgetting to believe in our Father in Heaven.

God sees our lives; He knew how our lives would be before we were even born. Nothing is a surprise to him. We must trust the Lord in all we do, believing that He has our lives in His hands. Trust is knowing everything will turn out alright when we ask God to help us. All the most important people in the Bible trusted God, and they were all blessed because of it. Maybe they did not trust Him at first; it probably took them a little time to trust Him. But they found out that it is easier turn to God. David trusted God, Joseph trusted God, Daniel trusted God, and Job trusted God. Moses, Paul, Shadrach, Mesach, and Abednego trusted God. These very important people put their trust in the Master of the universe to deliver them out of their situations. Asking for deliverance is not hard for the Lord; therefore, He wants us to ask and believe in Him.

Trust and know that God knows what to do, and how and when to do it. When He asks us to trust Him, He will use us to do things that do not seem sensible. But as I said, God knows what He is doing. To really trust God took me a long time—I kept giving my life to Him and taking it back. What was I doing? I could not fix my life myself by worrying, so I gave it to the one would and could fix it in His time. Trusting God to work in in His time makes sense because if He was to do it in our time, everything would go wrong, and we would not know to handle it. We can trust God.

As I said before, trust in God, no matter what. There is a song that says, "God is my everything, He's my joy in sorrow, He's shelter in the time of storm, God is my everything." So, trust Him. I almost forgot to mention Noah and His trust for God. He really needed to practice trust when God spoke to him, telling him to build an ark, for a flood was coming. God told Noah to go out and to get two animals of each kind, male and female. Well, I do not know whether or not Noah thought about that instruction for a while, but he followed God's command. You know, the people around Noah made fun of him; they laughed at him, called him crazy, and teased him to no end, but this did not discourage him. Noah trusted God, and he and his family was spared from the flood, while all who made fun of him lost their lives.

Trusting in God is not always easy, but think of this: God will not ask you to do something that He hasn't already equipped you to do. Trusting God is saying, "Alright, Dad, I know that You know what You are doing and I don't. I just have to learn to be patient and to realize that my blessings will come to me when I am ready to receive them." Trusting in the Creator of the universe is a great privilege because He chose you to believe that He can do anything. Therefore, trust God through tears, through pain, and sometimes through doubts. You may not always believe that what He says will happen, but you can then come and say, "My Father will see me through this. He knew this would happen; He also knew the strength that He put inside me." When we go through pain, it is a learning experience. That may sound funny or strange, but it is true. Going through the pain gives us more encouragement to believe in God, knowing that He will deliver us; then, we can give thanks—even for the pain, and especially for the deliverance. Our Father is worthy of the glory and praise.

Chapter 7

Praise God through the Pain and Tears

*P*raise God through pain and tears. Praise the Lord, glorifying Him and thanking Him for bringing His Son, Jesus, who gave His life for us. Although we go through trials that hurt us emotionally, as it is said, the Lord will not give us any more than we can handle. With His help, we all will overcome our trials. There is a song that says, "Hallelujah."

Anyhow, praise the Lord, no matter what. Praise Him even when you are hurting and feel like crying. I do not like to cry. I try to tough it out, although I have cried when alone. When I do, I ask myself, "What am I crying for?" When my mom passed to her new home, I did not cry, for I knew where she was going. Yes, it hurt to lose my best friend, and it hurt to lose my home, but I kept saying, "The Lord is in control." This I say, "Lord, I give You praise, for You know I spent a week in the park with no place to go. How did I get there?" Losing the house is a reverse mortgage; they wanted their money. I also was driving a 2013 SUV that I lost too. I am telling this secret because I wanted to give up, but I now give praise and thanks to the Lord for keeping me safe. I could have been attacked. My youngest son was a comfort to me. By the way, he was my trouble child, so see how God can bring good things out of bad? I gave God praise, for He helped me through my trials, and He sent a dear friend who let me stay at her home, which was already full.

I say all this to encourage you to keep on praising the Lord. He may not give you the answer you want when you want it, but do not stop praising Him. Give thanks to God in all things. Yes, when you are in emotional or physical pain, it is sometimes hard to say, "Thank you, Lord." But God is always waiting for that. Thank God when you are able to see another day, for you know there is a blessing headed your way. Sometimes pain is meant to strengthen you for what is to come. We are stronger than we think.

Chapter 8

Remember the Cross

*W*hen I think about the cross, I think about two pieces of wood. Through old and rough, those pieces of wood have great meaning, for our Lord and Savior died on them. Jesus, the Son of the Living God, shed His blood for all mankind on that cross. We know the story of how God sent an angel to tell Mary that she was highly favored by God and would give birth to the Savior of the world. We have heard how the three wise men did not find Jesus until he was two years of age. We then did not hear more about Jesus until he was twelve, when Mary and Joseph lost Him in the temple; that is where they found Jesus saying, "I must be about my Father's business." I believe Jesus knew then that He would pick up His life at thirty.

I wonder how Jesus was as a teenager. Did He pick up His clothes from the floor? Was He obedient to His parents? Did He like going places with His friends? We do not know how Jesus's life was as a human boy and young man, but we do know that He obeyed His heavenly Father and began His great work of spreading the Good Word.

At the age of thirty, Jesus started to teach, and along the way, many amazing things happened. Jesus had a cousin named John the Baptist. Jesus and John had a connection when Mary told John's mother she was with child. Within his mother's womb, John leaped. At the start of His ministry, Jesus wanted John to baptize him, but John did not feel worthy; however, he did what Jesus asked. Now Jesus was a humble and sweet person. Excuse me for this illustration, but it seems like Jesus was Clark Kent when he went under the water, and he was Superman when he came up. I may get some for that, but what did the Great I Am say? "This is my Son, in whom I am well pleased." We know that Superman is fictional, but Jesus is not. Jesus went around teaching, healing, and raising the dead; He did so many miracles that you probably would not be able to count them. Jesus did more in three years than anyone could do in a lifetime. I just do not understand how people could praise Jesus, welcoming Him to the city with gladness at one time, then turn on Him a little later.

The same people who were there screaming Jesus's name and yelling, "Hosanna in the highest," were there to crucify Him. But our Lord and Savior Jesus Christ was humble. They tormented Him as He walked toward the hill to be crucified. While He was carrying the heavy cross, no one help Him. They put a heavy crown of thorns on His head, and when He was on the cross, thirsty, they gave Him vinegar instead of water. They put up a sign that said "King of the Jews," thinking the sign was mockery and an insult, not knowing Jesus indeed was the King of the Jews. Jesus went through all of this, shedding His blood, while they laughed at Him and called Him nasty names.

However, the nails did not hold Jesus there; His love for all who were yet to be born held Him on that cross. No love can match that love. Had it not been for Jesus, where would we be? We owe Him all of our praise.

I think of how during all Jesus went through, He never stopped loving us. He asked the Father to take the bitter cup from Him, for Jesus did not want to go through this, but He did. It was the love He had for us that led Him to do so. Now I do think about Pontius Pilate, who saw no wrong that Jesus did but wanted nothing to do with His conviction. Why did Pilate wash his hands? He did not want Jesus's blood on his hands. My, my. .if.he only knew how powerful that precious blood was and how important it would be, he might not have wanted to wash it off.

I bring this to light to say that there is power in the blood of Jesus Christ. We should be grateful that He gave His life so that we could have life here on earth and the life He has already prepared for us in Heaven.

Chapter 9

Read and Study the Bible

The Bible is one of the most interesting books to read. These days, the Bible has been written in many languages, so there is no way we cannot understand what God's Word says. In the Scriptures, God gave many of His people a way to tell their stories of how they were blessed to be saved and to share how we also can be saved from our troubles. These stories inspire us to trust and believe in the Great I Am and His Son, King Jesus.

There is a song that says, "Read your Bible and pray every day, and you will grow." It may sound like a child's song, but it has a great meaning. We are God's children, and He wants nothing but the best for us. Reading the Bible and understanding what it says will help us believe more in God and share His truth with others. Talking with others about what we read will help us and them.

These days, we have all kinds of resources for finding a Bible that will fit our needs right now. What I mean by that is, you can understand God's Word, and not rewrite it for your pleasure. I said that so you will realize that everyone needs to understand that God's Word has one meaning. God is love, and He wants us to obey His Word and to be kind to one another. I was just saying this to make sure you understand the Bible; no matter what version you use, they all should have the truth of what God is saying.

When you read the Word, it is a reflection of the goodness of the Great I Am. We learn how the authors lived and how God delivered them. We can also learn how we can repent of our sins and live the lives God intended for us. Our ups and downs of life will be easy if we just remember how far the Lord helped those who wrote the Bible to help us. Study, read, believe, understand, and be thankful for God's Word, which keeps us strong.

Chapter 10

Gratefulness

$\mathcal{P}$salms 56:10 says, "The vows are upon me, oh God. I will render praises unto you." Verse 13 says, "For thou has delivered my soul from death will not deliver my feet from falling. That I may walk before God in the living light." We pray for deliverance from the things that might keep us down, but do we appreciate God's answer? We sometimes just say, "Lord, I need You," and when we feel that the prayer is answered, we relax and forget to praise God for want He has done. Don't you know that He already knows what we need spiritually and has already put into place what we need?

We must pray and praise the Lord, showing our gratefulness for what He has already done and what He will do. It is our duty to praise God, for He owes us nothing. We need to be grateful for His love and wisdom of knowing all that we need. We often take God granted. Through His love, we can see, breathe, hear, talk, think, and more. He laid out our lives even before we were a twinkle in our parents' eyes. Thank the Lord for all He has already placed in our future. He knows what we need, but He gives us a chance to ask Him and believe that He will provide.

To be able to wake up in the morning and plan our day is such a great gift. God gave His Son, Jesus, who sacrificed

His life, and He alone deserves our gratefulness. Be grateful for your life; do not wish for the life of someone else, for you may not even be able to handle it. God gave you and me the life He wanted us to live for Him, and He has equipped us to be a light for others.

When God opens our eyes in the morning, it is for a purpose and for His glory. So be thankful for everything He is doing in your life and have joy. Jesus is worthy to be praised.

This is the day that the Lord has made, and I will rejoice and be glad in it.

Each day you wake up is a blessed day. God prepares each day for all of us individually. Therefore, my blessing is not your blessing; this is why we have to thank God for ourselves. The ability to see, think, breathe, hear, speak, and move around is a blessing. There so many people who cannot do these things. You see, often, we look for the big blessings, those blessings that cost a lot, but you know what life costs? More than you can imagine.

Just think about Jesus and what He has done for us. We should thank God for His love, mercy, and patience, especially for us, His often ungrateful and sometimes crazy children. He planned our lives way before we got here, and He planned them according to the way He made us. He knew our manners and our personality, so He has planned our blessings specifically for each of us. What I mean to say is, God knows what we need, when we need it, and we can handle the great blessings He has for us.

So, each day is a blessing, and I thank God for it. When you say, "Thank you, Lord," it seems to make your day better.

Chapter 11

Encouragement

I am trying to encourage you and others. Many times in my life, I have been discouraged. Then I think about the goodness of my Jesus and all He has done for me. In life, the good can outweigh the bad if you just look at your situation with open eyes and an open heart. Like I said before, when you wake up in the morning and all of your body parts work, that is a blessing in itself. Think about last night—a lot of things went on in other parts of the world, in your city, in your state, and in your country; other people who went to sleep did not wake up, or something bad happened to them. Yet, you woke up in a bed, got up, and were able to do all you do every morning, for God kept you safe. That means He had plans for you today.

You know, our lives are not for us; our lives are for others to see Christ in us and how much of a good life we can have with God. No matter what you are going through, you can be an encourager. You and I are here to be good examples of believers going through difficulties. Oh yeah, we have problems, but as believers, we give our problems to the Lord. This is necessary, for I can't solve them, and you can't either. The light is not ours; it is the Lord's. Therefore, we are to trust Him, pray, read the Word, fast, and know that He will hear us and bless us. I know this can be hard sometimes, and no one is perfect. But with Jesus, we can do all things, for Christ strengthens us. I am encouraging you—and myself.

Just remember that the devil was once an angel, and one of the most beautiful in heaven. However, his head got too big, and he thought he could outdo God, the Creator. Well, Satan had to be brought back to reality. You cannot go beyond the Great I Am. So, God cast Satan out of heaven. What I am trying to say is, do not let Satan in your spirit, for he also knows your good and bad traits. Yet, you have the power to call on God and not give Satan any more power than he has, which is none if you believe in Jesus and call on His name, which is the greatest power of all.

Jesus is all power, but He is also love, mercy, and patience. I love music, and there was a song that said, "So let the sunshine in face with a grin, smilers new loose are frowners never win, let the sunshine in, open up your heart and let the sunshine in." Well, Jesus is that sun. I believe if you think about it, you have more to smile about than to frown about, don't you think so? Nobody said the rank would be easy, but with Jesus on board, it is a little easier to travel.

We are covered by Jesus's blood and His love. Through life, there are so many things that happen to us, and our Lord's presence makes them easier. What I am saying is, we owe Jesus praise, no matter what we are experiencing.

I love to refer to praise songs; to me, they are testimonies with music. "Jesus is the light of the world. He's my rock, my sword, my shield; He's my wheel in the middle of the wheel. Jesus is mine, mine, mine. Everywhere I go, I am so glad He is mine. So glad, here in Jesus's name." The are some lyrics of old but powerful songs I grew up on, and they remind me of His great love, both then and now.

My purpose of writing this book is to encourage someone who is looking down instead of up. God woke you up this morning, and He did not wake you up to be sad, looking back on old stuff from your past. He woke you up to see what He has for you in the future. Now is the time to recognize who He is and who comes to destroy what God has for you to do.

I thank God for the gift of life. John 3:16 says, "For God so loved the world for he gave his only begotten son for who so ever believe in him shall not perish but have everlasting life." This is true love. When you think about how much love went into Jesus staying on that cross, I mean, it boggles the mind and spirit. The love that Jesus had for us thousands of years ago, knowing what messes and trials we would get into, was so powerful that He gave His life so we could have an everlasting one with Him. Jesus loves us. When we want to cry about our lives and how they may not be going the way we want, just trust the Lord; give Him a chance to bless you His way, in His time. That blood Jesus shed covers us; yes, we experience difficult situations that make us wonder if we might get out, but guess what? We will.

Jesus. .Jesus. .do you know how powerful that name is? Jesus! Just say His name! Can you imagine how the enemy feels when he hears that powerful name? I am a living example of how just saying Jesus will keep you believing.

I have an example of this: I once was a school bus driver, and I was driving my students home one day. I had cross a railroad, and I needed to make sure the tracks were clear to cross. I started to move and stepped on the gas. While I was moving very fast, I saw the light turn red. I was still pretty far from the light, but I had to apply the brakes (which were air). As I was approaching the light, which was still red, the bus kept on rolling, so I slammed my foot on the brake and started calling on Jesus. He heard my cry, and the bus stopped just short of the crosswalk. Don't tell me He's not real.

Chapter 12

Through the Fire

*A*s I have stated before, I am writing this because the Lord asked me to do so. Do you know how hard it is to do something that the Master wants you to when you think you can't? Well, He would not have asked you to do something if He didn't know and believe that you could do it. God is so wonderful.

This is my testimony. I want to encourage those who think that when you make a mistake or do something wrong, your life is over; truthfully, your life is not over, and you are forgiven. I was born to a woman who did not want me; she was married to my dad, who was in the military. She was young, so when I think about her decisions, I now can understand. I was blessed to be with my grandmother, and as I understand, that marriage ended, and my dad met a God-fearing woman (well, she was young too). After he married this woman, he put me in her arms and said I was her baby. You would think that my life would be joyful all the time. .but it wasn't so. You see, my life did not turn out the way I would I have chosen. However, at age eleven, I gave my life to the Lord.

When I titled this book *Gone through the Fire, Came Out Unsinged,* I was thinking about the three Hebrew boys, Shadrach, Meshach, and Abednego, who were tossed into the fire that had been turned up seven times hotter than usual. Yet, when the one who threw them in the fire looked in at them, he was astonished. Not only did these three young men not burn up, but there was a fourth man in there with them. When they came out, only the ropes upon them had burned off, and they didn't even smell like smoke. How great is that?

My favorite scripture is Psalm 121, which says, "I will lift up my eye unto the Lord (hills) from which cometh my help my help cometh from the Lord." When I read that scripture, I feel comfort because I believe God has my back, my side, and my front. Therefore, I am covered. When God says, "I will be with you and will not forsake you," He means it. Do not forget that the Lord knows everything, so when our lives take a different direction, remember, this is not news to God. He already knew what would happen, and all you have to do is believe that He will see you through. .and He will.

There is a saying that says, "What does not kill you makes you stronger." Well, you are still here, so continue to thank the Lord for the strength He has given you. It is not your strength; it is from the Lord.

Chapter 13

God's Calling

When I think about my life, I remember that I wanted to be married but have no children, for I did not want to bring any children into this mean, cruel world. Well, things turned out differently. I had two sons, and I got married—I just changed my name. You know, God loves you, but when you go against what He has asked you to do, you have to see the spiritual light. He wanted me to understand that I went against His wishes. Although He loves me, He desired for me to see how I went against His wishes and to see what I did.

Well, I had two possibilities in my future of being my mother. I was so bitter and ran them off (you see, this had been my secret, and I wanted no one to know, but He did. Revealing this makes me strong and allows me to forgive myself). My two sons were meant to be here, but I came close to losing my life while giving birth to them. Still, this was all in God's plan. Even though some people think differently, God has plans our lives. I thank the Great Master for always being there, even though I did not know He was. I am thankful because His plan has made me who I am supposed to be.

We all have a calling on our lives, and let me tell you, whatever the Lord has given you to do, do it well. Perhaps you are to be a teacher, a preacher, a poet like the late great Maya Angelou, a reader of stories to children, or one who takes care of senior citizens. There are a lot of wonderful gifts our Lord has given us, and when He wakes them up within us, He expects us to use them for His glory. Use what He gives you—even if you are a stay-at-home mom, that is a great job in itself. Your self-worth comes from God and what He has given you to do. I have done some dumb things in my life, and now I wonder how I could have done certain things differently. I tell myself, *Well, it happened, and God knew about it, or He made it happen.* That should throw off the real righteous folk, making them ask, "What?" They might be blaming God. Well, He knew what was going to happen.

What I am saying is, I want to praise God. I want to praise His name, for He is holy and He is my Rock. I think I wrote that before, but in everything, I praise the Lord. Remember, the Lord loves us all. He is our Shepherd, and He sent His precious Son to heal us of all the things we go through. Just trust in Him, and He will give you your path. You can't go wrong or get lost when you use the Lord as your GPS.

I encourage you to give God a chance in your life, and through all things, always praise Him. Nothing that happens in your life will surprise Him. He wants to hear a "thank you," and when He does, He will know that you trust Him to see you through.

Chapter 14

Faith

*W*e all go through challenging things, but like I said, the Lord knows all. He knew what would happen in your life. It is important to start and end your day by praying and reading the Bible. His Word says that we should pray without ceasing. But when you pray, you must pray in faith, believing the Lord will see you through, for we walk by faith, not by sight. Hebrews 11:1 tells us, "Now faith is the assurance of things hoped for, the conviction of things not seen." We are to have faith knowing that God will see us through. Hebrew 11:6 says, "Without faith, it is impossible to please Him, for whosoever will approach Him must believe that he exists and rewards those who see him."

God is moved by our faith in Him, as well as by our praise. When we live a life of believing that the Lord knows and cares about what we need, it should be easy to believe that He will bless us. There is hope for those who are reaching out for peace of mind—it only comes from knowing Christ. Therefore, pray. In John 6:35, we learn that Jesus is the bread of life. Walk with Him as He walks with you, believing and trusting in Him, knowing that He will never leave you or forsake you. What a friend we have in Jesus (Gal. 5:22-25). Do not take His love lightly.

They went through to be leaders for Christ. We all go through difficult things—some more than others—but we have a covenant with Jesus, who died on the cross and shed His blood for our sins. What we go through is purposed to make us stronger and more grateful for our Lord. Even with all that we go through, He will not let anything happen to us. We owe praise to the Lord, and we must trust that He will not leave us, for He loves us too much. We are his children, and He is the best parent. We should worship Him, for no day is owed to us. When we wake up in the mornings and see a new day, starting out the day by saying, "Thank you, Lord," will make our day much better. Ephesians 2:8 says, "For by grace you have been saved through faith, and this is not your own doing; it is a gift of God."

Our great God of mercy always knows what is going to happen before it does, and He will not allow us to go through more than we can handle. During my challenges, I learned that I was blessed with more strength and courage than I had thought. God knows what we will gain from overcoming our problems. No one said that the road of life would be easy, but it is so wonderful to know that we have a holy Father. I call Jesus my spiritual brother, although He is in all authority and gives us great love through His blood that He shed on the cross.

Praise and give thanks to God, no matter what is going on in your life. He will give you peace during the storm, so do not stop praying, having faith, and praising Him. Faith and worship are what move God. There is a song that says, "Hallelujah, now don't let your troubles get you down, when Satan blocks your way, stand right up and say, 'Hallelujah,' anyhow." Trust and praise are what God looks for in our lives. He will bless you at the right time, for He knows what He is doing. Trust the Lord with all your heart, and you will be blessed. Don't you know that He loves you and wants you to have the best in life? Give thanks in all that you do and all that you experience. Through it all, God is there, and He will hear and bless you.

I think about many great people who are now with the Lord, such as Reverend Billy Graham. I heard him say on an interview that he hoped he would hear God say, "Well done, my faithful son." I watched Reverend Graham through the years—he was one of God's great warriors. My late pastor, Andrew Crouch, wrote great songs and sang them all over the world. I grew up in his father's church, but I did not know all he had gone through to be where God placed him. These wonderful obedient people praised God through everything.

Chapter 15

Power in the Blood

I am leaving you with this note. I love the movie *Ben Hur,* for it tells of how a special man encountered Jesus. Ben Hur came from a well-known and well-to-do family. One day, officials were parading to the city, so his sister went to the rooftop to get a better view. Well, an accident happened, and a horse got spooked and almost threw off an official. They were blamed. This family lost everything because of some people thinking they were more superior than others. Ben Hur's mother and sister were put in prison. Judah Ben Hur was a friend of the centurion, yet this did not matter. The family lost their home, as well as their status in the community.

Meanwhile, Jesus was about to come into His assignment that God had prepared for him. A friend of Ben Hur's family and Judah's girlfriend went to hear Jesus teach. Meanwhile, Judah somehow was taken as a slave on a ship of the centurions. He did, however, come to see Jesus. When Jesus offered him a drink, the centurion tried to stop Him. Even then the great power of Jesus was there, and the centurion was afraid of Him. Judah Ben Hur was a hero saying a top official. He considered him as his son. But Judah wanted to help his people; he been a well-known top chariot racer.

Meanwhile, it was discovered that his mother and sister had leprosy and had been put into a leper colony. Judah found a procedure to help them, along with a family friend. He found out that Jesus was in the area, and what road to take there to see Him, for he heard about how Jesus could heal. He found Jesus on His way to the cross; it really hurt him. This was the man who wanted to help him. He needed Jesus's help, and he tried to get to Him, but the centurion would not let him.

I tell you all this to let you know that when Jesus was crucified, His blood ran down to the cave where Judah's mother and sister were rushed to because of the people not wanting them there. But the blood went straight to where it was supposed to cleanse, and it did. *Ben Hur* is only a movie, but it has a great meaning. God does move in mysterious ways, right? I just wanted to share this. We are all covered with the blood of Jesus. PS: Note that the blood did not even go in the cave where they were; it went by the cave. See how powerful the blood of Jesus is? Praise the Lord.

What a movie! Those who made it had to be blessed. Oh, did I say that the blood went by the cave, not in it, and they were still clean? We are then clean. When you believe in Jesus and let Him in, He will cleanse everything within you. Therefore, don't forget to praise Him. We were on Jesus's mind when He was up there on that cross, and His love was there for us all.

Chapter 16

Happiness in Christ

I have had sad days, I have had bad days. I've had warm days, upside-down days, and backwards days. But when I think about want God has done for me, even my crazy days seem mild. I become happy when I think about His goodness, His love, and His forgiveness, for I then know that everything is going to become better. There so many people who are down and in worse positions than me. Thinking about the plans God has for me, I know they are good. He makes me happy, and I start laughing about the strange things that had gotten me down.

We do not always have a laughing day, but when you think about how Jesus sacrificed His own life so that we could have life more abundantly, it makes you smile and say, "Thank you, Lord." Being sad changes our situation, and being happy will change it as well, for it helps us to look forward to the wonderful blessings God has for us. Being sad takes a toll on our physical being, and God desires that we are healthy, both spiritually and physically. Did you know that it takes more muscles to frown than to smile? Therefore, let's smile, even when we are hurting. Think of a good song and pray. Yes, life can sometimes be hard. I know because I am in pain all the time, but I pray and trust the Lord.

I have not always been a smiler. People would often think that I was just looking mean, but when you are hurt, whether emotionally or physically, your pain will show. However, instead of offering prayer, they offered critical words. When you turn to the Lord and talk to Him, He understands your pain and will give you something to smile about. I love the song "Jesus Is All the World to Me." Jesus won't make fun of you or say mean words. He will give you peace and love. It is so amazing that He will give you the love for the ones who made you feel bad, allowing you to show them love and patience. Trust and believe in Jesus, and He won't disappoint you. Praise and trust Him. When you rise the next day, due to the mercy of the Lord, you will see a great change in your life. Wow, what a grand feeling! You will look back and say, "Why was I so upset about a little thing like that?" Whatever is troubling you, give it to Him and watch Him work it out. Pray, trust, and believe, and your blessing swill flow.

My whole reason for writing this passage—and this entire book—is help someone else believe in God, knowing how much He is love. It blows my mind how He knew me before I even "was." I was meant to be here, for He chose me to be here. So, if He has chosen me, it means that He is going to take care of me. I thought I was a mistake, but no, I was not put here by chance. I was born late, unwanted by my birth mother, but all of this was in God's plan. Whew! He is amazing, and His plans are perfect, even when they do not work with ours.

I say this to explain that it took me many years to figure out why I was here, then many more years to wonder what I was supposed to do here. It was easy, but I made it hard. Still, God loved me. I guess He said, "She will get it in due time." I want to encourage you to listen to the Lord, for He does talk to you in quiet times. With me, He gives me a song in the middle of the night to let me know that He is there. The song is just the right one for the right time. Be encouraged to listen. Be encourage to talk, for He wants to hear from you. Be encouraged to hold on. Be encouraged to write. Be encouraged to sing, for He loves to hear your voice.

No matter what goes on in life, do not stop being encouraged. Faith is encouragement and stepping out. Sometimes, you just have to say, "I am going to do this, no matter what." But most of all, be encouraged in Jesus, for He is your source of love, faithfulness, patience, and forgiveness. He is the great provider. Be encouraged to trust the Lord. When you have tried everything else and have gotten over the frustration, have a talk with Jesus; tell Him all about your troubles, for He hears your fainted cry and will answers by and by.

Jesus is the rock of salvation, so go to the rock. All will be well with your soul. Christ is the answer, so trust the Lord today. He will make a way. These are words from songs sending the Word from the best book ever—the Bible. God's Word is so wonderful. When I used to sing in the choir and on the praise team, the words of these songs helped me, and they will also help you when you feel down. Like I said before, I am very intimate with the Lord when He speaks to me through songs. He will also wake you up in the middle of the night to talk to you.

Perhaps He will ask you to pray for someone, which will help you too. Believe it or not it, if you forget about yourself and think about someone else instead, He will draw you closer to Himself. When you bless others, you can see the blessings come to you as well. Everyone has something bothering them, and they all need prayers. To see someone else praying for them from the heart, this helps them find their breakthrough. Jesus is listening for your prayer all the time. Keep dreaming for a better life with Jesus, and He will bless you with all that you need and then some. He is very generous! Look how we are blessed to rise every day, and before we go to sleep at night, we have so much to be thankful for that Lord has seen us through during the day.

I just wanted to remind you—and myself—that the Lord is our Shepherd and we shall not want. He knows everything that goes on, especially in our lives. He is always around those of us who truly believe in Him, and even though silence may sometimes come, we can hear from Him. Do not stop praising Him if you want His attention. Give Him praise, for Jesus is alive and is always working for us! So, keep on believing and praising His name. He will answer you with a great blessing at the right time. Trust Him.

CPSIA information can be obtained
at www.ICGtesting.com
Printed in the USA
BVHW082345301121
622869BV00009B/300

9 781662 831980